Name________________________________

MW01043144

Day 1

1. If 19 – 9 = 10,
   then 9 + ____ = 19.

2. If 15 – 8 = 7,
   then 8 + ____ = 15.

Day 2

Spencer was angry. He did not want to do chores. He thought chores were not fun. He wanted to play outside instead. His friends were waiting for him in the yard.

1. Why was Spencer angry? He had to do chors
2. What did he think of chores? He thought they weren't
3. What did he want to do? Play outside
4. Who was waiting in the yard? His frinds

Day 3

Unscramble the letters to fill in the missing words.

1. Riding a bike instead of taking a car to work reduces
   air (iar) pollution.
2. Fertilizers used on lawns can trickle into the
   water (tewar) supply.
3. Be sure to throw garbage into trash cans instead of on the ground. Littering pollutes our land (ndal).

Day 4

An **event** is something that happens. A time line shows in what order events happen.

1. Draw a time line of events that have happened to you this year at school.

Name________________________________

Week #39 Assessment

1. Circle each way you can help our planet.

   A. Do not litter.

   B. Reuse many things.

   C. Turn off lights when you leave a room.

   D. Walk instead of driving.

   How many sentences did you circle? ________

2. Design a bumper sticker for a car with a message about helping our planet.

3. Write about ways to recycle or reuse one item in the picture.

____

____

Grade 1

Carson-Dellosa Publishing, LLC
Greensboro, North Carolina

Credits
Content Editors: Elise Craver, Christine Schwab, Angela Triplett
Proofreader: Karen Seberg

Carson-Dellosa Publishing, LLC
PO Box 35665
Greensboro, NC 27425 USA
carsondellosa.com

ISBN 978-4838-1235-9
04-215151151

Table of Contents

Introduction

Common Core First Grade 4 Today is a perfect supplement to the first-grade classroom curriculum. Students' skills will grow as they support their knowledge of math, language arts, science, and social studies with a variety of engaging activities.

This book covers 40 weeks of daily practice. Each day will provide students with cross-curricular content practice. During the course of four days, students complete questions and activities in math, language arts, science, and social studies in about 10 minutes. On the fifth day of each week, students complete a writing assessment that corresponds with one of the week's activities.

Various skills and concepts in math and English language arts are reinforced throughout the book through activities that align to the Common Core State Standards. The standards covered for the whole week are noted at the bottom of that week's assessment page. For an overview of the standards covered, please see the Common Core State Standards Alignment Matrix on pages 5–8.

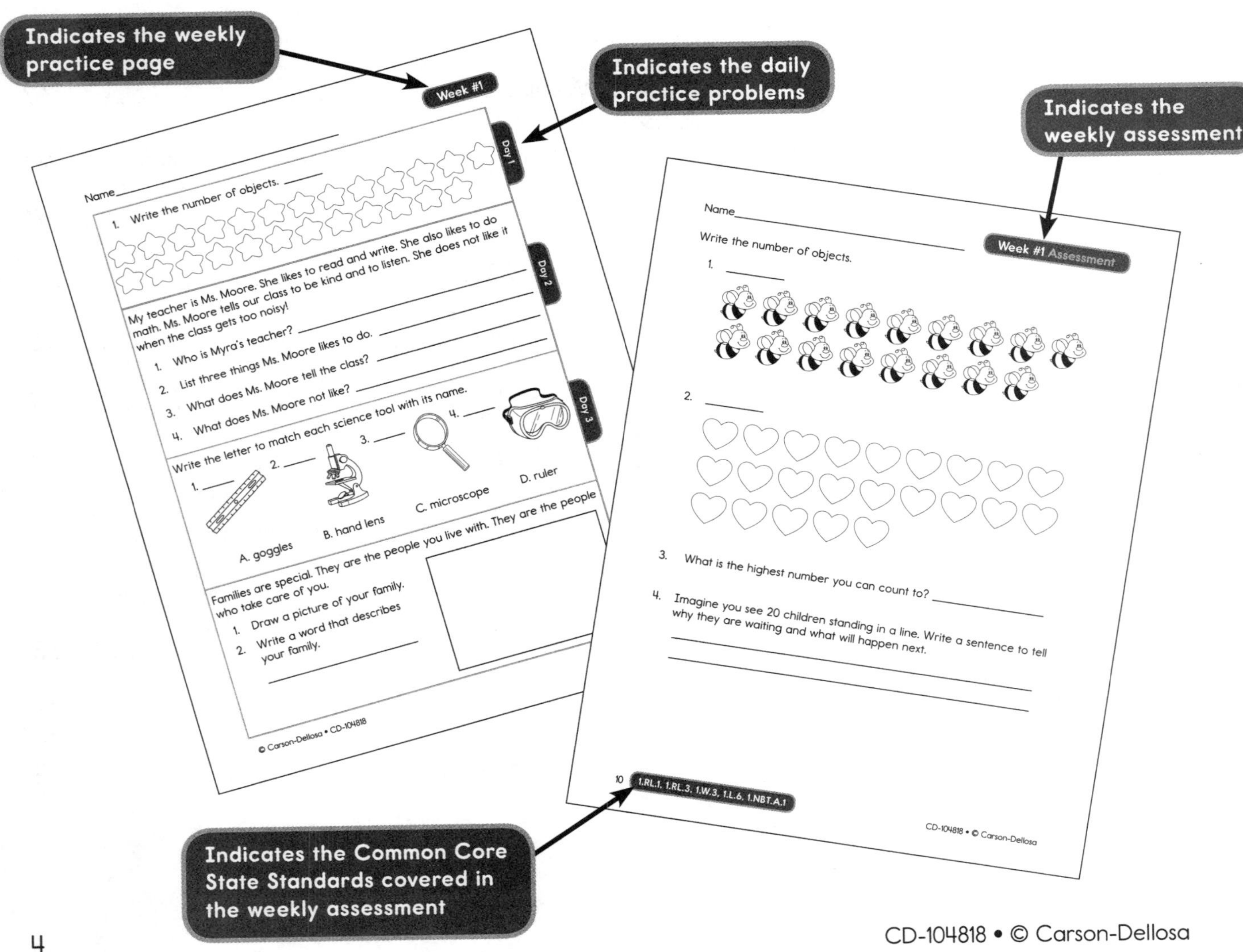

Common Core State Standards Alignment Matrix

Language Arts

STANDARD	W1	W2	W3	W4	W5	W6	W7	W8	W9	W10	W11	W12	W13	W14	W15	W16	W17	W18	W19	W20
1.RL.1	●								●				●						●	
1.RL.2									●				●						●	
1.RL.3	●								●				●						●	
1.RL.4													●							
1.RL.5																				
1.RL.6																				
1.RL.7																				
1.RL.9																				
1.RL.10																				
1.RI.1			●		●		●				●				●		●			
1.RI.2											●				●					
1.RI.3																				
1.RI.4			●														●			
1.RI.5																				
1.RI.6																				
1.RI.7																●				
1.RI.8																				
1.RI.9																				
1.RI.10																				
1.RF.1																				
1.RF.2		●						●												●
1.RF.3		●												●						●
1.RF.4																				
1.W.1				●					●			●			●		●			
1.W.2			●		●		●			●	●								●	●
1.W.3	●	●						●					●	●	●	●		●		
1.W.5																				
1.W.6																	●			
1.W.7											●									
1.W.8						●														
1.SL.1																				
1.SL.2																				
1.SL.3																				
1.SL.4																				
1.SL.5																				
1.SL.6																				
1.L.1		●		●		●		●		●		●				●				
1.L.2		●				●												●		
1.L.4						●						●		●			●			
1.L.5		●	●		●		●			●	●			●				●	●	●
1.L.6	●															●				

W = Week

Common Core State Standards Alignment Matrix

Language Arts

STANDARD	W21	W22	W23	W24	W25	W26	W27	W28	W29	W30	W31	W32	W33	W34	W35	W36	W37	W38	W39	W40
1.RL.1			•				•				•		•				•		•	
1.RL.2			•				•				•		•				•		•	
1.RL.3			•				•						•							
1.RL.4																				
1.RL.5																				
1.RL.6																				
1.RL.7																				
1.RL.9																				
1.RL.10																				
1.RI.1	•				•				•						•					
1.RI.2	•				•				•						•					
1.RI.3		•						•												
1.RI.4															•					
1.RI.5																				
1.RI.6																				
1.RI.7																				
1.RI.8																				
1.RI.9																				
1.RI.10																				
1.RF.1																				
1.RF.2																		•		
1.RF.3										•										
1.RF.4																				
1.W.1				•							•		•		•	•			•	
1.W.2			•				•	•		•		•			•				•	•
1.W.3	•				•				•								•	•		
1.W.5		•				•											•			
1.W.6														•						
1.W.7																				
1.W.8			•																	
1.SL.1																				
1.SL.2																				
1.SL.3																				
1.SL.4																				
1.SL.5																				
1.SL.6																				
1.L.1				•				•		•	•	•								•
1.L.2								•						•						•
1.L.4		•	•			•	•			•				•		•	•		•	
1.L.5	•				•															
1.L.6												•								

W = Week

Common Core State Standards Alignment Matrix

Math

STANDARD	W1	W2	W3	W4	W5	W6	W7	W8	W9	W10	W11	W12	W13	W14	W15	W16	W17	W18	W19	W20
1.OA.A.1				•					•								•			
1.OA.A.2																				
1.OA.B.3		•										•								
1.OA.B.4																				
1.OA.C.5			•																	
1.OA.C.6					•						•			•						
1.OA.D.7						•														
1.OA.D.8										•			•						•	
1.NBT.A.1	•							•												
1.NBT.B.2																				
1.NBT.B.3																				
1.NBT.C.4																				
1.NBT.C.5																				
1.NBT.C.6																				
1.MD.A.1																		•		
1.MD.A.2															•					
1.MD.B.3							•													
1.MD.C.4																				
1.G.A.1																				
1.G.A.2																				
1.G.A.3																•				•

W = Week

Common Core State Standards Alignment Matrix

Math

STANDARD	W21	W22	W23	W24	W25	W26	W27	W28	W29	W30	W31	W32	W33	W34	W35	W36	W37	W38	W39	W40
1.OA.A.1	•				•															
1.OA.A.2											•				•					
1.OA.B.3																				
1.OA.B.4																				
1.OA.C.5																				
1.OA.C.6																				
1.OA.D.7																				
1.OA.D.8												•							•	
1.NBT.A.1																				
1.NBT.B.2		•								•										
1.NBT.B.3				•																
1.NBT.C.4			•											•						
1.NBT.C.5						•							•				•			
1.NBT.C.6																•				
1.MD.A.1																				
1.MD.A.2							•													•
1.MD.B.3								•												
1.MD.C.4									•									•		
1.G.A.1																				
1.G.A.2																				
1.G.A.3																				

W = Week

Name________________________________

Day 1

1. Write the number of objects. ______

Day 2

My teacher is Ms. Moore. She likes to read and write. She also likes to do math. Ms. Moore tells our class to be kind and to listen. She does not like it when the class gets too noisy!

1. Who is Myra's teacher? ________________
2. List three things Ms. Moore likes to do. ________________
3. What does Ms. Moore tell the class? ________________
4. What does Ms. Moore not like? ________________

Day 3

Write the letter to match each science tool with its name.

1. ______

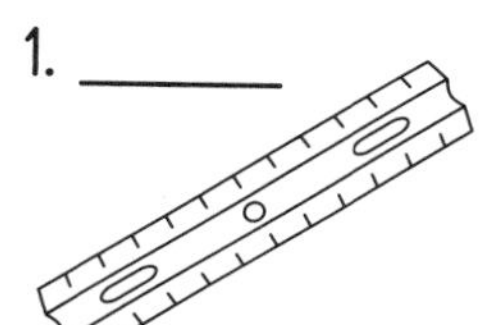

2. ______

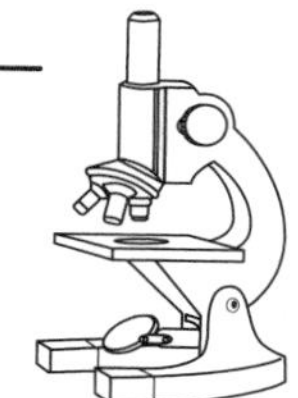

3. ______

4. ______

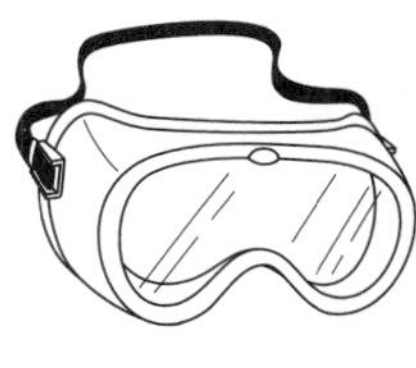

A. goggles B. hand lens C. microscope D. ruler

Day 4

Families are special. They are the people you live with. They are the people who take care of you.

1. Draw a picture of your family.
2. Write a word that describes your family.

____

Name___________________________________

Write the number of objects.

1. __________

2. __________

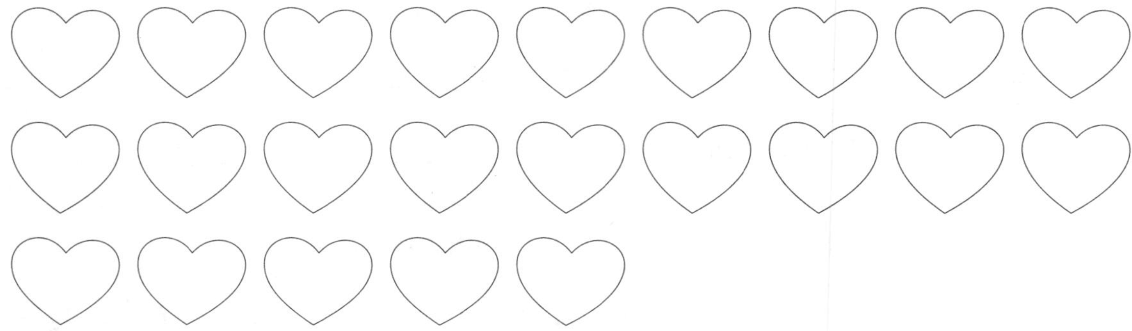

3. What is the highest number you can count to? ________________

4. Imagine you see 20 children standing in a line. Write a sentence to tell why they are waiting and what will happen next.

____

____

Name________________________________

Week #2

Day 1

1. If 7 + 2 = 9, then 2 + 7 = ________.
2. If 5 + 3 = 8, then 3 + 5 = ________.

Day 2

1. A sentence starts with a capital letter. Use a capital letter.

   (my) ________________ dog takes a bath.
2. Circle the picture whose name has the **short a** sound.

3. Place a period at the end of a sentence that tells something.

   The dog and the cat have fur
4. Circle the correct words. cit cat buth bath

Day 3

1. Tia has sorted the animals into two groups. Fill in the top of the chart to show how she sorted them.

butterfly	cat
owl	worm
bee	snake
eagle	alligator

Day 4

Friends do not all look the same. They can have different skin colors and hair colors. They can be boys or girls.

1. Draw a picture of yourself and a friend. Tell about one thing that is the same.

____

Name________________________________

1. Write the first word of the sentence. Use a capital letter.

   (she) __________ will bring her video game.

   (peter) __________ hit the ball out of the park.

2. Read each sentence. Write a period at the end of each sentence.

   My teacher read a story to us

   The doctor tapped my knee

3. Circle the correct words.

   nap nop

   lig leg

4. Do you have a pet? ________

5. Write a complete sentence about your pet or a pet you have known.

   ____

   ____

Name________________________________

Day 1

1.
```
   8
   9
 + 1
 ---
```

2. 7 + 6 + 3 = ______

Day 2

Rice is a food. Many people in the world eat rice a few times a day. Almost all rice is grown in ponds. The rice crops need a lot of rain to grow.

1. Who eats rice? ____________________
2. Where is rice grown? ____________________
3. What do rice crops need? ____________________
4. Write a sentence about a time you ate rice. ____________________

Day 3

Draw a line to match each type of safety equipment to its use.

1. fire extinguisher	A. to clean up spills
2. latex gloves	B. to put out fires
3. paper towels	C. to protect the hands
4. goggles	D. to protect the eyes

Day 4

Community helpers are people who help make your community a good place to live.

1. Look at the pictures. Circle the community helpers who keep you safe. Draw a triangle around the community helpers who keep you healthy.

Name________________________________

Week #5 Assessment

1.

2.

4	4
4	3
+ 3	+ 6

3. I see 7 pink fish, 3 purple fish, and 4 orange fish in an aquarium.

   How many fish are in the aquarium? ________ fish

4. Imagine the aquarium is in your room at home. Tell two things you could do to take good care of the fish.

   ____

   ____

   ____

Name____________________________________

Day 1

1. Is this sentence **true** or **false**?

   If 10 + 8 = 18, then 8 + 10= 18. ____________

Day 2

1. Capitalize each proper noun.

   pascal __________________ virginia ________________

   walsh __________________ utah __________________

2. Add **-e** to turn each short vowel word into a long vowel word.

   rip__ pin__ dim__ bit__

Day 3

Complete the sentences. Unscramble the letters to fill in the missing words.

1. You use your nose to ____________________ (lmsel).
2. You use your eyes to ____________________ (ese).
3. You use your ears to ____________________ (erah).
4. You use your tongue to ____________________ (satet).
5. You use your hands to ____________________ (cuhto).

Day 4

A **citizen** is someone who lives in a community or neighborhood. A good citizen helps her neighbors. A good citizen keeps his community clean.

1. Draw a picture that shows how you can be a good citizen.

Name____

1. Read the story. Find and circle seven proper nouns.

Kit wanted it to snow. She put on her boots and went outside. It was cold. The sky was gray. But, there was no snow.

Kit heard a sound. She looked up. Her cat Fluffy was sitting in a tree. She wanted to come down.

"Here, Fluffy, come here!" Kit called.

Fluffy jumped down. Kit picked her up. She saw a snowflake on her head. She looked at the sky. It was snowing!

2. Which two names did you circle?

____________________ ____________________

3. Why are they proper nouns?

____

4. Write a sentence to tell what your name means. Ask your teacher to help you find out if you do not already know.

____

____

Name________________________________

Week #7

Day 1

1. Write the time shown on the clock.

____

Day 2

Sharks live in the ocean. They have been here for thousands of years. In the ocean are more than 350 kinds of sharks. Some sharks have big teeth. Others have small teeth.

1. Where do sharks live? ________________________
2. How long have they been here? ________________________
3. How many kinds of sharks are there? ________________________
4. What size are sharks' teeth? ________________________

Day 3

1. You want to observe how quickly the moon travels across the sky. Circle the tools that might help you.

magnifying glass　　telescope　　compass

pencil　　camera　　notebook

Day 4

Rules are made to keep children safe at school. Rules also keep order. Read each sentence. Write a ✓ by each sentence that shows a good rule.

_______ 1. Run in the hallway.

_______ 2. Raise your hand to ask a question.

_______ 3. Keep your hands and feet to yourself.

_______ 4. Throw trash on the playground.

Name________________________________

Week #7 Assessment

1. What can a telescope help you learn about?

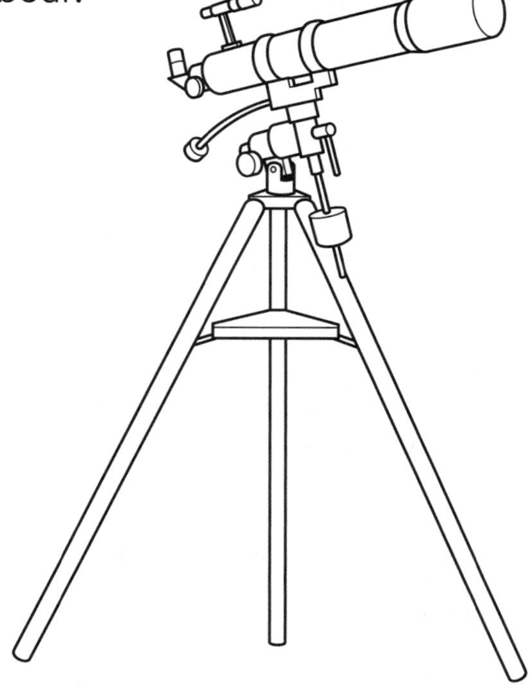

A. weather

B. rainbows

C. stars

D. birds

2. You want to learn more about the sun. What question might you ask?

____

____

3. You want to learn more about spiders. How could you find facts about spiders? Write a complete sentence.

____

____

Name________________________________

Week #8

Day 1

1. Draw a line to match each number word to its number.

twenty-eight	14
fourteen	5
five	28

Day 2

Some verbs are action words. They show movement. Circle each verb.

1. Yuri rides his bike.
2. Mia smells the food.
3. Claire holds the fork.
4. Taylor sees her mom.

Blends are two or more letters that make sounds together. They can start words. Circle the blend in each word.

5. blue
6. blot
7. blip
8. blur

Day 3

Write **F** if the sentence is a fact and **O** if the sentence is an opinion.

1. _____ Apples taste good.
2. _____ Apples are a fruit.
3. _____ Apples grow on trees.
4. _____ An apple tree is pretty.

Day 4

A **right** is to be free to do something. A **responsibility** is an action you must take.

1. Place each word from the word bank in the correct box.

follow rules	learn	play	read

Right	Responsibility

Name________________________________

Circle **right** or **responsibility** to complete each sentence.

1. It is your (right, responsibility) to go to school.
2. It is your (right, responsibility) to do your best each day at school.
3. It is your (right, responsibility) to live where you wish.
4. It is your (right, responsibility) to be a good neighbor.

5. Draw a picture about a time you were not responsible.

6. Write two sentences telling about your picture.

____

____

____

Name________________________________

Week #9

Day 1

1. Leslie buys 12 gallons of lemonade for the party. She serves 9 gallons of lemonade during the party. How many gallons of lemonade does Leslie have left?

   Leslie has _______ gallons of lemonade left.

Day 2

Liv wanted to do one thing. She wanted to ride a horse. She loved horses. She read horse books at the library. She drew horses in art class. She had horse pictures in her room.

1. What did Liv want to do? ______________________________
2. What kind of books did she read at the library? ____________
3. Where did she draw horses? ____________________________
4. How do you know she loves horses? Write a sentence. ________

   ____

Day 3

1. Look around you. Write down four observations you have made.

   ____

   ____

   ____

   ____

Day 4

Conflict is a disagreement over something.

1. Draw a picture of a time you had a conflict with someone.

2. Write a sentence to tell how you solved the conflict.

   ____

Name____

Week #9 Assessment

1. Nassim bought 15 stamps. He used 10 stamps. How many stamps does Nassim have left?

   Nassim has __________ stamps left.

2. Rachel rode her bike for 4 hours on Saturday. She rode her bike for 3 more hours on Sunday. How many hours did Rachel ride her bike altogether?

   Rachel rode her bike for __________ hours altogether.

3. Write a sentence to tell what you think Rachel did after her bike ride on Sunday.

   I think Rachel ____

   ______________________________ because ________________________

   ____.

Name___________________________________

Week #10

Day 1

Write the number that makes the number sentence true.

1. 9 + _______ = 16

2. _______ + 7 = 13

Day 2

1. **Adjectives** are describing words. Circle the picture that matches the adjective.

hot

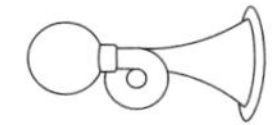

2. Write an adjective to describe a ball. ______________________________

3. One vowel team is **-ay**. It makes the **/ā/** sound.

Write three words that rhyme with **day**? ________ ________ ________

Circle each **-ay** vowel team. May play okay Ray

Day 3

Animals in the cat family have four legs, fur, and whiskers. They are meat eaters.

Write **C** next to each animal that is a cat. Write **N** next to each animal that is not a cat. Then, tell why it is not a cat.

1. _____ tiger ______________________________

2. _____ eagle ______________________________

3. _____ turtle ______________________________

Day 4

Use a word from the word bank to complete each sentence.

December	Friday	January	Saturday

1. __________________ is the first month of the year.

2. __________________ is the day before Saturday.

3. __________________ is the last month of the year.

4. Most children do not go to school on __________________.

Name____

1. Draw a line to match each adjective to the picture it describes.

tall 

cold 

slow 

fast 

2. Circle each **-ay** vowel team.

lay clay stay hay say

3. Look at the picture. Write three things that you see. The first sentence has been started for you.

The giraffe has a __________ neck. ____________________________________

____

____

Name____________________________________

Day 1

1. 15
 − 8
 ____

2. 14
 − 4
 ____

Day 2

The **ostrich** is a large bird. It has long legs and a long neck. It has a large body. An ostrich can grow to be up to nine feet (2.74m) tall. It is taller than a man. It is so big that it cannot fly.

1. What is an **ostrich**? ____________________
2. How tall can an ostrich grow? ____________________
3. What is an ostrich taller than? ____________________
4. Write a sentence to explain why an ostrich cannot fly. __________
____

Day 3

Matter is anything that takes up space and has mass.

1. Circle the objects made of matter.

   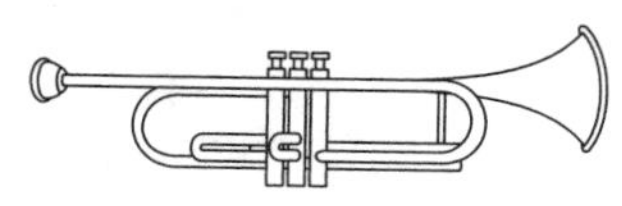 

Day 4

A **tradition** is something that a family may do every year to celebrate a special date. For example, many families have a holiday tradition. They may eat special foods or sing special songs.

1. Draw a tradition that you and your family have.

2. Write a sentence to tell about your picture. ____________________
____

Name____________________________________

Week #11 Assessment

1. Matter has shape. Write the letter to match the object with its shape.

A. rectangular prism   B. cylinder   C. sphere   D. cone

2. Matter can have different textures. Name an object that is smooth.

____

3. Matter comes in different sizes. Name an object that is large.

____

4. Choose two objects. Write two sentences to tell how the objects are alike.

____

____

____

Name____

Week #12

Day 1

1. If 5 + 3 = 8, then 3 + 5 = ______.
2. If 7 + 2 = 9, then 2 + 7 = ______.

Day 2

A **contraction** is two words that become one. A contraction has an apostrophe.

1. is not = isn't What letter is replaced by the apostrophe? __________
2. do not = ______________

The letters **-ow** can sound like the **/ow/** in **now**.

3. **Now** rhymes with __________, __________, and __________.
4. Circle the two pictures whose names have the **/ow/** sound.

Day 3

Fill in the blank with one of the states of matter: **solid**, **liquid**, or **gas**.

1. Water is a ______________. It takes the shape of its container.
2. A wooden block is a ______________________. It does not change shape.
3. Oxygen is a ____________________. It fills the space it is given.

Day 4

In 1620, the Pilgrims set sail on a ship called the *Mayflower*. The ship had over 100 people on it. It was very crowded. There was not enough food. Many people got sick. There were many bad storms during the trip. After two months, the Pilgrims landed in America.

1. Circle the words that describe life on the *Mayflower*.

   sickness   crowded   too much food   bad storms   fun

2. How long was the trip to America?

   ____

Name____

Use a word from the word bank to complete each sentence.

food	*Mayflower*	months	sick

1. The Pilgrims came to America on the ____________________.
2. The trip to America took two ____________________.
3. There was not enough ____________________ on the ship.
4. Many people became ____________________.

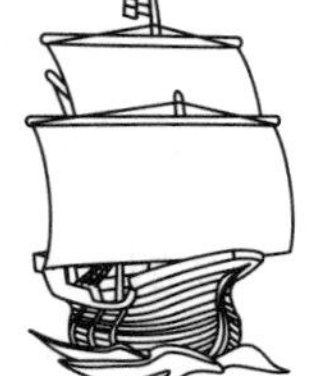

5. Draw a picture of the Pilgrims on the *Mayflower*.

6. Would you like to have been a passenger on the *Mayflower*? Write a sentence to tell why or why not.

____

____

Name____ **Week #13**

Day 1

Write the number that makes each number sentence true.

1. _______ + 5 = 19

2. 7 + _______ = 18

Day 2

Ming asked her grandmother a question. She asked if she could have a teacher to help her learn to act. Ming wanted to learn how to have fun onstage. Her grandmother said it was a good idea. Her grandmother called an acting teacher. Ming was happy!

1. What did Ming ask her grandmother? ____________________
2. What does Ming want to learn? ____________________
3. What did Ming's grandmother do? ____________________
4. How did Ming feel? Write a sentence. ____________________

____

Day 3

Draw a line to match each word with its definition.

1. float	A. when an object stays on top of a liquid
2. matter	B. when an object goes below the surface of a liquid
3. sink	C. anything that takes up space and has mass

Day 4

A **culture** is a group of people who share the same music, food, and types of clothes. They speak the same language. They may live near each other.

1. What do people in your culture like to wear?
   Draw a picture of the clothes.

2. What do people in your culture like to eat?
   Draw a picture of the food.

Name____

1. Write the number that makes the number sentence true.

   ______ + 2 = 17

2. Hector picked 11 apples. He gave 3 to his neighbor. How many apples does Hector have left?

   Hector has ______ apples left.

3. Mrs. Wolf baked 18 cupcakes. Puffy, the cat, ate 4. How many cupcakes does Mrs. Wolf have left?

   Mrs. Wolf has ______ cupcakes left.

4. Write a sentence to tell what you think Mrs. Wolf did with the cupcakes she had left.

   ____

   ____

Name____

Week #14

Day 1

1.
$$\begin{array}{r} 15 \\ +\ 3 \\ \hline \end{array}$$

2.
$$\begin{array}{r} 6 \\ +\ 5 \\ \hline \end{array}$$

Day 2

Some words are strong adjectives. Make the adjective stronger.

1. That dog is **big**!

   That dog is **huge**!

   The doll had a ________________ pair of shoes.
   (small)

Some words have more than one meaning. Write another meaning for **ring**.

2. ring – on a finger

   ring – ____

Day 3

Fill in the missing letters. Use the clues to figure out the three forms of energy.

1. L___gh___ energy comes from the sun and helps us to see objects.

2. Hea___ energy gives us warmth. It comes from sources like the sun and fire.

3. S___ ___nd energy comes from vibrations. We use our ears to hear it.

Day 4

Christmas, Hanukkah, and Kwanzaa are holidays that some families celebrate in December. Each holiday has special foods, traditions, and music.

1. Draw a picture of a holiday you celebrate in December.

2. Write a sentence to tell about your picture.

   ____

Name____

1. Draw a line to match each adjective to the stronger adjective.

soft	giant
hot	beautiful
tall	fluffy
pretty	burning

2. Some words have more than one meaning. Write the second meaning for each word.

   A. close – nearby

   close – ________________________________

   B. row – things in a straight line

   row – ________________________________

   C. park – to stop the car in a spot

   park – ________________________________

3. Write about your favorite toy. Use three or more adjectives to describe it.

____

____

____

Name______________________________

Day 1

1. How many fish long is the fishing rod?

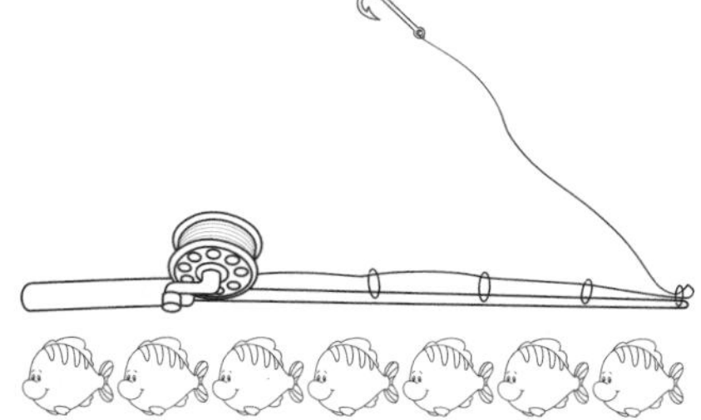

The fishing rod is _______ fish long.

Day 2

Maple trees are filled with sweet sap. To get to the sap, holes are drilled into the trees. The second step is to hang a bucket on each tree. The sap falls into the buckets. The buckets are made of metal. When sap falls into the buckets, it makes a *ping, ping* sound. The buckets are full at the end of the day.

1. Where does the sap drip from? ______________________________
2. What is the second step? ______________________________
3. What are the buckets made of? ______________________________
4. When are the buckets full? ______________________________

Day 3

1. Circle the animal that can move faster.

   turtle   cheetah

2. Circle the object that can move faster when pushed down a hill.

   sphere   cube

3. Circle the object that can move faster when pulled.

   empty wagon   wagon full of bricks

Day 4

1. Draw a line to match each symbol to its meaning.

   railroad crossing

   school crossing

          recycle

Name____________________________

1. Draw a picture of a roller coaster that goes up and down and has a loop. Write an **F** by the places where you think the roller-coaster cars would go faster. Write an **S** near places the cars would slow down.

2. Do you like to go fast or slow on a roller coaster? Explain your answer.

____

____

3. Write two complete sentences about a time you rode an amusement park ride.

____

____

____

____

Name________________________________

Day 1

1. Draw a line to show how you and 1 friend can equally share this cookie.

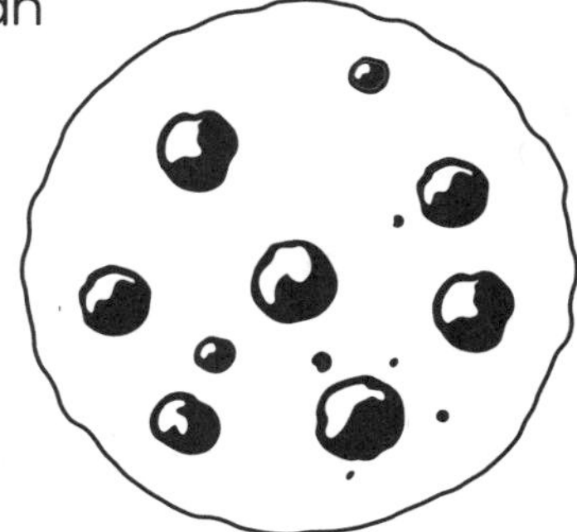

Day 2

A **conjunction** joins two words, phrases, or sentences.
Example: We went to the pond **and** saw the ducks.

1. The conjunction is **and**. Write a sentence with **and**.

____

A verb is an action word. It can be in the past, present, or future tense.

Example:
Past: played Present: play Future: will play

2. Past: kicked Present: __________ Future: __________ __________
3. Past: baked Present: __________ Future: __________ __________

Day 3

1. Look at how the objects are being moved. Write **push** or **pull** under each picture.

A. 

B. 

C. 

D. 

______________ ______________ ______________ ______________

Day 4

Martin Luther King Jr. was a peaceful man. He wanted people to use kind words to solve conflicts. He wanted people to work and play together fairly.

1. What did Martin Luther King Jr. want people to use to solve conflicts?

____

2. How did he want people to play and work?

____

Name________________________________

Martin Luther King Jr. wanted all people to be treated with kindness.

1. Circle the words that show kindness.

   nice gentle mean unfair fair caring

2. What do you think the word **fair** means?

   ____

3. Draw a picture of a time you were not treated fairly.

4. Write two complete sentences telling about your picture.

   ____

   ____

   ____

Name______________________________

Week #17

Day 1

1. Claire ate 1 banana for breakfast. She ate 7 grapes for snack. How many pieces of fruit did she eat in all?

   Claire ate ______ pieces of fruit in all.

Day 2

Haiku are short poems. Haiku are from Japan. They are sometimes about nature. A haiku has 17 syllables. It has three lines. The first line has five syllables. The second line has seven syllables. The third line has five syllables.

1. Where are haiku from? ______________________
2. How many syllables are in a haiku? ______________________
3. How many lines are in a haiku? ______________________

Day 3

Use a word from the word bank to complete each sentence.

down	Earth	gravity	moon

1. ________________ is a force that pulls objects toward the center of ________________.
2. Because of gravity, what goes up must come ________________.
3. The ________________ revolves around Earth because of gravity.

Day 4

A **globe** is a round model of Earth. A **map** is a flat picture that can show the world, a city, or a neighborhood.
Look at the pictures. Write **map** or **globe** under each picture.

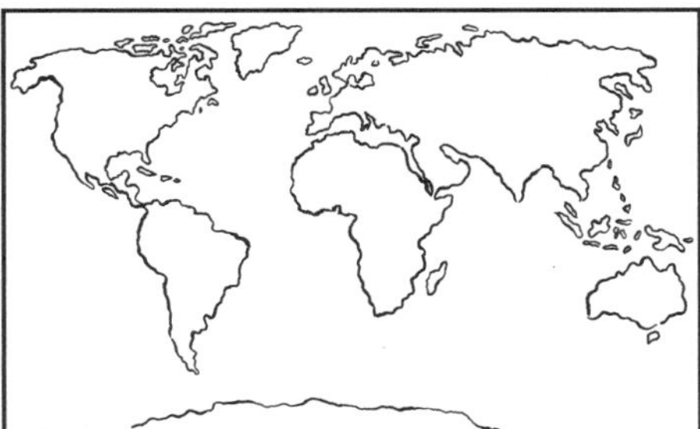

1. ____________ 2. ____________

3. What do both of these things show? ______________________

Name____________________________________

1. Draw a line to match each problem to the correct answer.

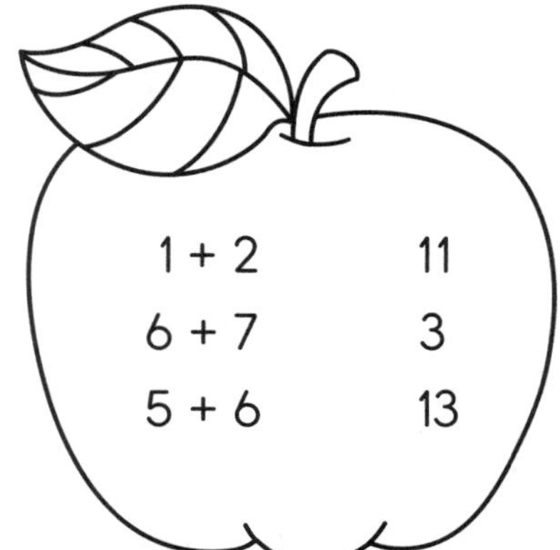

2. What is your favorite fruit?

____

3. Write a sentence to tell why it is your favorite fruit. Then, type your sentence on a computer.

____

____

____

____

Name____

Week #18

Day 1

1. Number the objects as follows: 1 = long; 2 = medium; 3 = short.

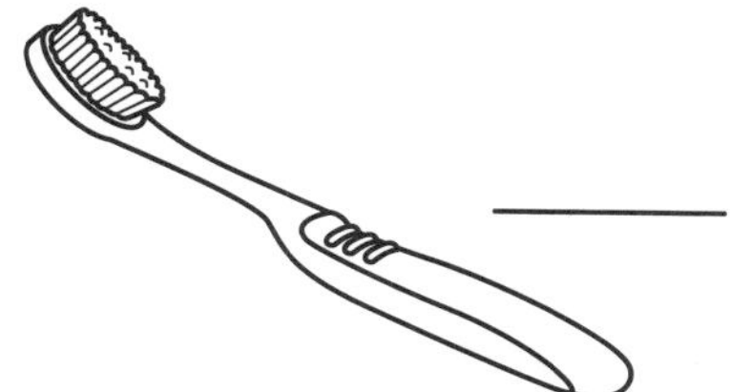 ______ 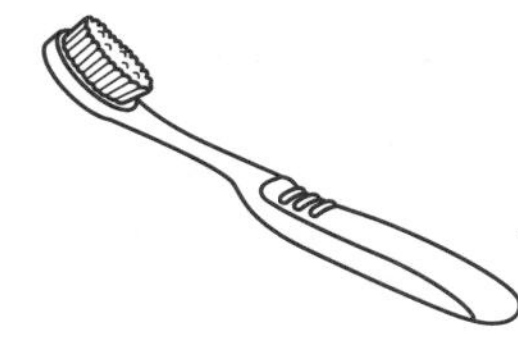 ______ 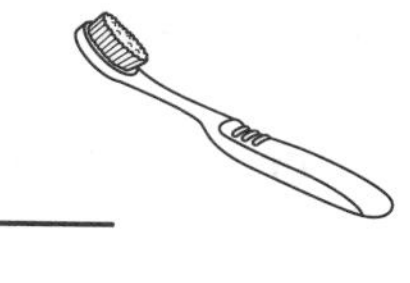 ______

Day 2

An exclamatory sentence shows a lot of feeling. Add an exclamation point to the end of each sentence.

1. That is great
2. I am happy for you
3. This is wild

A **compound** word is two words joined together. They make one word. Write each compound word.

4. back + pack = ________________
5. sun + shine = ________________

Day 3

1. Look around your classroom. List items you think are magnetic and items you think are not magnetic.
2. What is the same about the items in the Magnetic column?

____

____

Magnetic	Not Magnetic

Day 4

Look at the picture. Circle the correct answer.

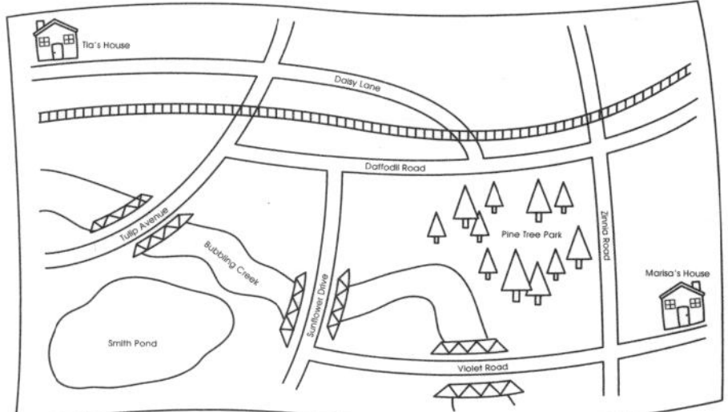

1. This is a (globe, map).
2. This is a picture of (a town, the world).
3. How many houses do you see? one two
4. Is there a railroad in the town? yes no

Name_____________________________________

1. Place an exclamation point at the end of each sentence.

   A. My dad and I were amazed

   B. The boys could not believe their eyes

   C. I won the award

2. Draw a line to match the words that make each compound word.

can	noon
skate	get
after	board
for	not

3. Imagine you are at a zoo. You are watching the monkeys. One of them looks friendly. He runs up to you.

   Write two or three sentences about what happens next. One of the sentences should tell about a feeling. Place an exclamation point at the end of that sentence.

Name________________________________

Day 1

Write the number that makes each number sentence true.

1. ______ + 3 = 14

2. 6 + ______ = 15

Day 2

Grandma Kate moved into our house last month. She needed us to help her. She has a cane. It helps her walk. She has glasses. They help her see. She has a hearing aid. It helps her hear.

1. Why did Grandma Kate move in? ____________________

2. How does her cane help? ____________________

3. How do her glasses help? ____________________

4. How does her hearing aid help? ____________________

Day 3

Write **L** if the object is living. Write **N** if the object is nonliving.

1. _____ rock

2. _____ apple tree

3. _____ bird

4. _____ fish

5. _____ bike

6. _____ doll

Day 4

Read each sentence. Write **globe** if you would use a globe. Write **map** if you would use a map.

__________ 1. To find a friend's house

__________ 2. To find the Pacific Ocean

__________ 3. To find the nearest park

__________ 4. To find North America

__________ 5. To find a local library

Name____

1. Circle the things that are living.

2. Choose one living thing. Tell how you know it is a living thing.

____

____

3. Choose one nonliving thing. Tell how you know it is a nonliving thing.

____

____

Name________________________________

Day 1

1. Draw lines to show how you and 3 friends can equally share this cake.

Day 2

Blends are two or more letters that make sounds together. A blend can be at the end of a word. Circle each ending blend. Write a word that rhymes.

1. bump

   It rhymes with ______________.

2. camp

   It rhymes with ______________.

One vowel team is **-oa**. It makes the **/ō/** sound. Circle the **-oa** vowel teams.

boat float oat goal

Day 3

1. Circle the plants.

apple tree	turtle	grass
sunflower	lettuce	caterpillar

2. Give three more examples of plants.

_______________ _______________ _______________

Day 4

A **compass rose** is a symbol on a map. It shows the cardinal directions of east, west, north, and south. Use the compass rose to answer the questions.

Name one thing that is each direction.

1. west of you ______________
2. north of you ______________
3. south of you ______________
4. east of you ______________

Name____

1. Complete the picture with **E**, **S**, and **W**.

Circle the correct answer.

2. What does this picture show?

   A. a map

   B. a compass rose

   C. a globe

3. What direction is the opposite of east?

   A. west

   B. south

   C. north

4. Think of a person who would need to use a compass rose. Write a sentence to explain how he would use it.

____

____

Name____________________________________

Week #21

Day 1

1. Ana typed for 7 hours. She typed for 5 more hours later. How many hours did Ana type in all?

   Ana typed for _______ hours in all.

Day 2

Ladybugs are from Europe. They came to America more than 100 years ago. Ladybugs live in many different places. They like forests. Ladybugs do not like the cold. Ladybugs hide in warm places in winter. They rest under rocks and logs.

1. Where are ladybugs from? ______________________________
2. When did they come to America? ______________________________
3. Where do ladybugs like to live? ______________________________
4. What happens when it gets cold? ______________________________

Day 3

1. Circle the animals that hatch from eggs.

   birds   turtles   people   dogs

2. Circle the animals that fly.

   bats   whales   birds   people

Day 4

People can live in the country or rural areas. People can live in the city or urban areas. Look at the pictures.
Write **rural** or **urban** under each picture.

1. 

   ____

2. 

   ____

3. 

   ____

4. ______________

5. Would you like to live in the city or the country? ____________________

Name____

1. Richie had 8 pencils. His friend gave him 5 more. How many pencils does Richie have now?

   Richie has ________ pencils now.

2. Cara has 4 cousins on her mom's side. She has 7 cousins on her dad's side. How many cousins does Cara have in all?

   Cara has ________ cousins in all.

3. How many cousins do you have? ________

4. Tell about something you have done with one of your cousins or family members. Use the name of your family member in the sentence.

   ____

   ____

   ____

   ____

   ____

Name________________________________

Week #22

Day 1

1. Circle each set of 10 objects. Write the total amount of tens and ones.

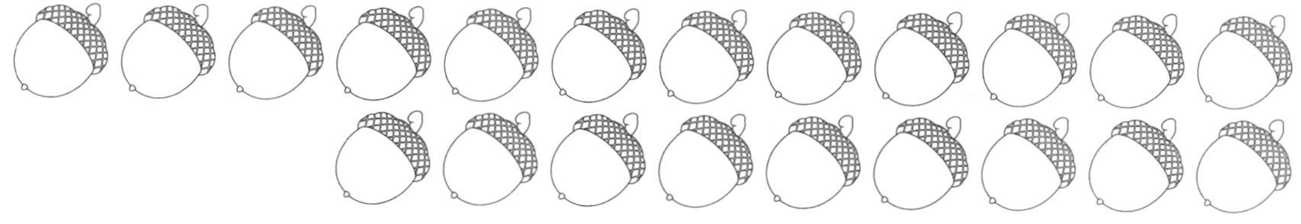

_______ tens _______ one

Day 2

Homophones are words that sound the same. They look different. They have different meanings.

Write a sentence with each homophone.

1. be ________________________________

2. bee ________________________________

3. **Qu-** sounds like **/kw/**. **Q** is almost always followed by **u**. Circle each **qu-**.

   quit   queen   quack

Day 3

Circle **true** or **false** for each sentence.

1. Animals help plants through pollination. true false
2. Plants help animals by making oxygen. true false
3. Animals give off carbon dioxide that plants use to make food. true false

Day 4

A landform is any part of Earth's surface. A landform can be a mountain, a valley, or a river. Look at the picture. Follow the directions.

1. Color the mountains brown.
2. Circle a valley.
3. Color the river blue.

Name____

1. Draw a line to match each pair of homophones.

ant	high
wrap	aunt
hi	by
buy	rap

2. **Kn-** sounds like **/n/**. Circle each **kn-**.

knee knife knock

3. **Ph-** sounds like **/f/**. Circle each **ph-**.

photo Phillip phone

4. **Wh-** sounds like **/hw/**. Circle each **wh-**.

wheel who where

5. Write a silly sentence with a pair of homophones from question 1. Then, read your sentence to a friend. Write another sentence together.

____

____

Name_______________________________________

Week #23

Day 1

1. $$\begin{array}{r} 24 \\ +\ 5 \\ \hline \end{array}$$

2. $$\begin{array}{r} 32 \\ +\ 4 \\ \hline \end{array}$$

Day 2

Ahmad is in a big room. It is on the top floor of his house. It is his attic. It is dark and dusty. Webs are in the corners. Ahmad finds a light. He pulls the string.

1. Where is Ahmad? ______________________________
2. What is the attic like? ______________________________
3. What are in the corners? ______________________________
4. What did Ahmad find? ______________________________

Day 3

Use a word from the word bank to complete each sentence.

bee	birds	flowers	skunks

1. A ____________________ has a stinger to protect him from predators.
2. ____________________ have colorful petals to attract insects.
3. Some ____________________ have strong beaks to crack open seeds.
4. ____________________ are black and white to warn other animals.

Day 4

The **climate** of a place is the usual weather in that area. Deserts are hot, dry places. Mountains are usually cold places. Rain forests have rainy climates.

1. Circle things you would find in the desert.

   cactus spiders snow snakes forests

2. Circle things you would find in the mountains.

   trees snow bears skiers camels

3. Circle things you would find in a rain forest.

   snow green plants frogs cactus monkeys

Name____

Week #23 Assessment

1. Write the letter to match each animal to the body part that helps her survive.

________ duck	A. strong back legs
________ fish	B. webbed feet
________ grasshopper	C. layer of blubber
________ whale	D. gills

2. Draw a good place for a green insect to hide. Color your drawing.

3. Explain why your drawing shows a good hiding place for a green insect.

____

____

____

____

Name________________________________

Day 1

Write **<**, **>**, or **=** to make each statement true.

1. 59 ◯ 39

2. 44 ◯ 44

Day 2

1. Write the correct types of words to complete each column.

Noun person, place, thing, or idea	**Verb** action word	**Adjective** describing word
apple	run	small

Day 3

Write the letter to match each baby with the adult.

1. ____ 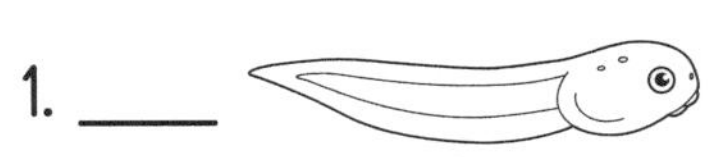

2. ____ 

3. ____

A. 

B. 

C. 

Day 4

A **natural resource** is something people can use in many ways. Natural resources come from Earth. Trees are natural resources.

1. Circle the things that are made from trees.

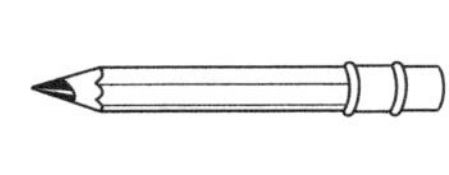

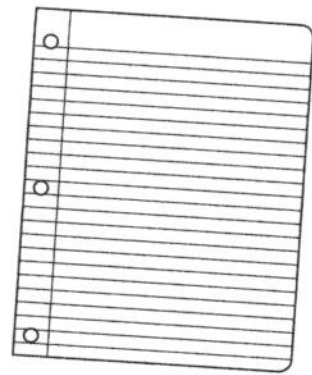

2. Name something else that is made from trees. ____________________

Name____

Circle the best answer.

1. A natural resource is something people use that ______________.

   A. is made of metal

   B. comes from Earth

   C. is made by humans

2. Which is an example of something that is made from a tree?

   A. a trumpet

   B. a drinking glass

   C. a pencil

3. Draw something that is made from a natural resource.

4. Trees are good for the environment. They help keep our air clean. They provide homes for animals. Should trees be cut down to make things?

   Write two sentences giving your opinion on using trees to make things. Then, share your sentences with a friend.

   ____

   ____

   ____

   ____

Name________________________________

Week #25

Day 1

1. Greg's yard has 11 trees. In the spring, 5 of the trees have flowers. The rest do not. How many of the trees do not have flowers?

   In Greg's yard, ________ of the trees do not have flowers.

Day 2

Trash is in landfills. A **landfill** is a big pile of waste. Paper is in landfills. Plastic is in landfills. Landfills make gas. We can recycle. When we recycle, the waste is used again. We do not have to put all trash in landfills.

1. What is a **landfill**? ________________________________
2. What is in landfills? ________________________________
3. What do landfills make? ________________________________
4. What happens when we recycle? ________________________________

Day 3

Name the habitat that is being described: **desert**, **tundra**, or **rain forest**.

	Animals	Plants	Climate	Habitat
1.	arctic hares, polar bears	arctic moss	very cold, dry	
2.	lizards, coyotes	prickly pear cactus	often hot, little rain	
3.	monkeys, tree frogs	rubber tree	very rainy	

Day 4

When we **recycle**, something used is made into another material. We can recycle plastic, cans, glass, and paper.

1. Draw items in the recycle box that can be recycled.
2. Choose one of the items you drew and tell how it can be used again.

   ____

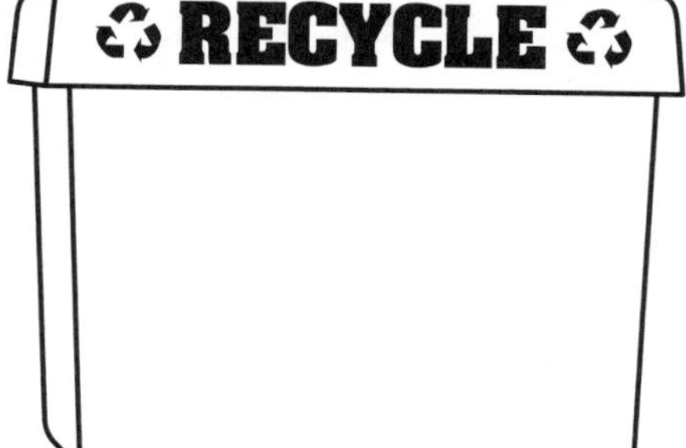

Name____

1. Out of a class of 18 students, 7 students have curly hair. How many students do not have curly hair?

   In this class, ______ students do not have curly hair.

2.
$$\begin{array}{r} 61 \\ +\ 8 \\ \hline \end{array} \qquad\qquad \begin{array}{r} 54 \\ +\ 3 \\ \hline \end{array}$$

3. Kim has 47 baseball cards. Gabe has 6 baseball cards. How many more baseball cards does Kim have than Gabe? Circle the correct answer.

   A. 15 B. 41 C. 62 D. 30

4. What do you collect? Why? Complete the sentence.

   I collect ____

   ________________________________ because ________________

   ____

   ____.

Name____

Write the number that is 10 less than the number shown.

1. 39 ______ 2. 46 ______

Day 1

A **prefix** is a part of a word. It is at the beginning.

1. Draw a line to match each prefix to its correct meaning.

dis-	before
un-	not
re-	not
pre-	again

Day 2

1. Number the pictures in the order that an egg would become a butterfly.

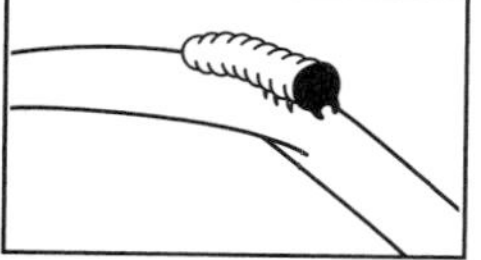    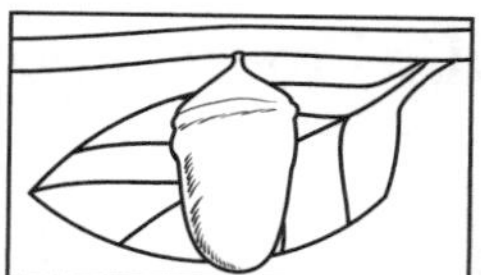

_____ _____ _____ _____ _____

Day 3

People work to earn money. Your occupation is the job you have to earn money.

1. Draw a picture of the job you would like to have when you grow up.

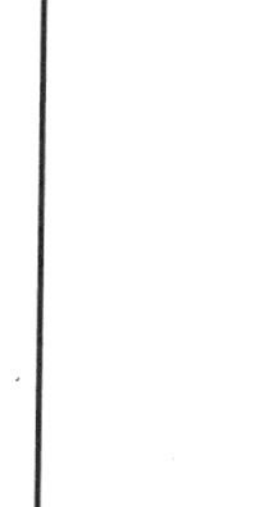

2. Write a sentence to tell about your picture.

____

Day 4

Name________________________________

1. **Pre-** means **before**. Write what the word means.

   preheat ______________________________

2. **Dis-** means **not**. Write what the word means.

   dislike ______________________________

3. **Re-** means **again**. Write what the word means.

   replay ______________________________

4. **Un-** means **not**. Write what the word means.

   unhappy ______________________________

5. Think of something you dislike. Tell what it is and why you dislike it. Then, read your story to your friends. Ask them what they think.

   ____

   ____

   ____

Name______________________________

Week #27

Day 1

1. How many cubes long is the toothbrush?

The toothbrush is _______ cubes long.

Day 2

Josie and Paws play with yarn. Josie tosses up the yarn. Paws jumps for it! Josie rolls it on the floor. Paws gets ready to pounce! Josie and Paws are good friends. Paws likes it when Josie brushes his fur. It makes Paws purr.

1. Who is Paws? ______________________________
2. What does Josie do with the yarn? ______________________________
3. What does Paws like? ______________________________

Day 3

Use a word from the word bank to complete each sentence.

bones	heart	lungs	muscles

1. Your ______________________ give your body its structure.
2. You use your ______________________ to move body parts.
3. Your ______________________ are used to breathe.
4. Your ______________________ pumps blood through your body.

Day 4

Abraham Lincoln was the 16th president of the United States. Martin Luther King Jr. was a preacher. They both wanted peace and fairness for everyone. Use the words from the word bank to compare the two men.

fair	peaceful	preacher	president

1. Place each word from the word bank in the correct column.

Abraham Lincoln	Both	Martin Luther King Jr.

Name________________________________

1. Use a word from the word bank to label each body part on the person.

elbow	eye	foot	hand	knee	nose

2. What are some things on your body that grow or change? Answer in a complete sentence.

____

____

Name________________________________

Week #28

Day 1

1. Write the time shown on the clock.

__________ 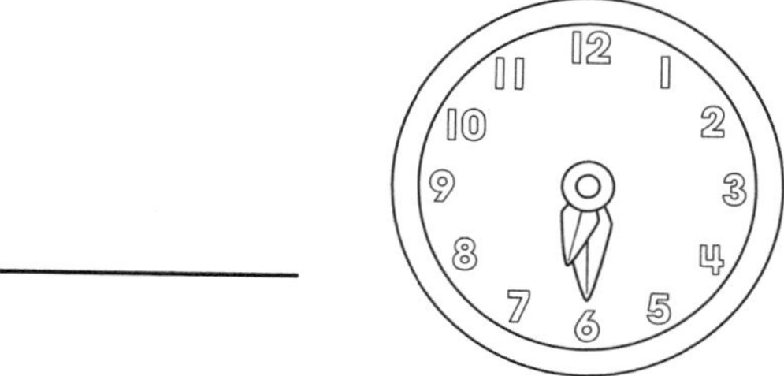

Day 2

The names of days and months are proper nouns. They are capitalized. Rewrite each word, beginning with a capital letter.

1. march __________________
2. february __________________
3. thursday __________________
4. saturday __________________

Write a question mark at the end of each asking sentence.

5. When will Ryan get home
6. Where is he

Day 3

Write **T** for true or **F** for false.

1. _____ The sun circles around Earth to make day and night.
2. _____ Earth circles around the sun to make day and night.
3. _____ Earth rotates around on its axis to make day and night.
4. _____ When it is day on one side of Earth, it is night on the other side of Earth.

Day 4

Needs are things that people need to survive, such as healthy food and fresh water. **Wants** are things that people would like to have but do not need them to live. Read each item. Write **W** if it is a want. Write **N** if it is a need.

_____ 1. baseball _____ 2. banana

_____ 3. candy _____ 4. bread

_____ 5. home _____ 6. cell phone

_____ 7. milk _____ 8. TV

Name____

Week #28 Assessment

Circle the best answer.

1. A need is

   A. a new toy.

   B. a new puppy.

   C. something you have to have to live.

2. A want is

   A. something you would like to have.

   B. something that keeps you alive.

   C. both A. and B.

3. Draw two wants.

4. Draw two needs.

5. Write three sentences explaining the things you would need to take along on an overnight camping trip.

____

____

____

____

Name____________________________________

Week #29

Day 1

1. Look at the tally chart. How many more people like purple than like orange?

Favorite Colors		
Orange	Purple	Yellow
III	~~IIII~~ II	~~IIII~~ I

Purple is liked by ______ more people.

Day 2

Sheepdogs came from England. They have long fur, so they need to be brushed often. They are strong dogs and love to work. They need a lot of activity. Sheepdogs like to play and run outside.

1. Where are sheepdogs from? ____________________
2. What needs to be done to their fur? ____________________
3. What do they love? ____________________
4. What do they like? ____________________

Day 3

Name what season each month falls in.

1. January ____________________
2. July ____________________
3. October ____________________
4. April ____________________

Day 4

Goods are the things that people buy. **Services** are things that people do for you that you pay for. Read each sentence. Write **good** or **service** on the blank line.

____________ 1. My mom bought cookies at the store.

____________ 2. My sister got a haircut at the salon.

____________ 3. The dentist cleaned my teeth.

____________ 4. My brother bought a new movie.

Name________________________________

Week #29 Assessment

1. Look at the tally chart. What color of hair do the most people have?

   The most people have __________ hair.

Hair Color		
Brown	Black	Blonde
𝍸 𝍷𝍷𝍷𝍷	𝍸 𝍷	𝍷𝍷𝍷

Books Read on Vacation by the Perez Family

Mario	
Caitlyn	
Sam	
Reese	

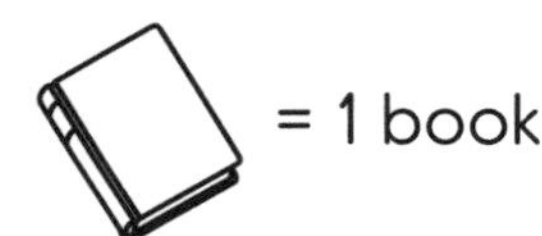

2. The Perez family read books during their vacation. Who read 6 books?

   ____

3. How many books did the family read altogether? ____________________

4. Write a sentence to tell about what your family did on a vacation.

   ____

   ____

Name________________________________

Week #30

Day 1

Write the value of each number.

1. 15

_______ ten

_______ ones

2. 23

_______ tens

_______ ones

Day 2

-Ew makes the sound **/ōō/** as in **few**. Add **-ew** to each blend.

1. fl___

2. st___

3. gr___

An **apostrophe** shows belonging. Add an apostrophe before **s**.
Example: Amy's cat has stripes. The cat belongs to Amy.

4. Shanes dad washed windows.

5. His dads towel was wet.

6. Moms car windows were dirty.

Day 3

Fill in the missing vowels to complete facts about the sun.

1. The sun provides l___ght to help us see.
2. It provides h___ ___t to keep animals warm during the day.
3. Plants use energy from the sun, along with carbon dioxide and water, to make f___ ___d.
4. Solar energy can be turned into electricity. We can use that power for electronics, such as c___mput___rs.

Day 4

A buyer is someone who buys something with money. A seller is a person or a store with something to sell.

1. Draw a picture of something you would like to buy.

2. Draw a picture of something you would like to sell.

Name____

Week #30 Assessment

1. **-Ew** makes the sound **/ōō/** as in **stew**. Add **-ew** to each blend.

   d________ fl________

2. **-Ue** makes the sound **/ōō/** as in **due.** Add **-ue** to each blend.

   bl________ gl________

3. **-Oo** makes the sound **/ōō/** as in **food.** Add **-oo** to complete each word.

   m________d t________l

4. **-Oo** makes the sound **/o͝o/** as in **book.** Add **-oo** to complete each word.

   l________k t________k

5. Add apostrophes to show belonging.

   Colbys father met him at the bus.

   I ate Arifas lunch by mistake.

   Matthew likes Lolas coat.

6. Talk to a friend. What is your friend's favorite day of the week? Why? Use the information to write a short story.

   ____

   ____

   ____

   ____

   ____

   ____

Name_______________________________

Week #31

Day 1

1. Anna had 6 marbles. Brad had 6 marbles. Chelsea had 4 marbles. How many marbles did Anna, Brad, and Chelsea have altogether?

_____ + _____ + _____ = _____

Anna, Brad, and Chelsea had _______ marbles altogether.

Day 2

Bridget looks at her kite. A breeze spins her kite around! It flies into a tree. The kite is stuck! Natalie runs over to help Bridget get her kite out of the tree. They tug at the string, and the kite falls out of the tree. The two girls look at each other and laugh. What a windy day!

1. What happened to Bridget's kite? ____________________
2. What did Natalie do? ____________________
3. What did the girls do to get the kite down? ____________________
4. What kind of day was it? ____________________

Day 3

1. How many moons does Earth have?

____

2. Use three adjectives to describe what the moon looks like.

____________________ ____________________ ____________________

Day 4

Technology changes over time. Look at the phones. Which of these phones came first? Which came last? Write **1**, **2**, or **3** to order how the phones have changed over time.

1. ☐  ☐  ☐ 

Name____________________________________

  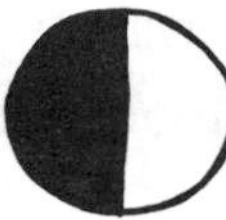  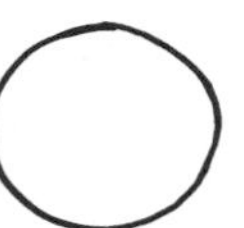 

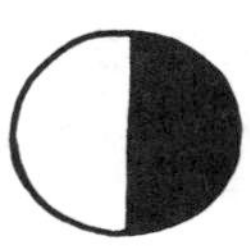 

1. Circle the picture of the missing moon.

A.  B.  C. 

2. The moon is what 3-D shape?

A. circle B. cube

C. pyramid D. sphere

3. Would you like to go to the moon? Why or why not?

____

____

____

____

____

Name____

Week #32

Day 1

Write the number that makes the number sentence true.

1. ______ – 2 = 14

2. 17 – ______ = 11

Day 2

To, **two**, and **too** each mean something different. Use the correct word in each sentence.

1. We went __________ the house.
2. There are __________ kids in the yard.
3. We will play at the house __________ .

A **pronoun** takes the place of a noun. Write the correct pronoun in each sentence.

4. Lily sits in a chair. __________ has a big pillow.
5. Mario goes to the store. __________ rides his bike there.

Day 3

1. Describe the weather this morning.

____

____

____

____

Day 4

To **manufacture** something is to make it in a factory. Look at the pictures.

1. Circle the things that are manufactured.

2. Name one thing in your room that is manufactured.

____

____

Name____

Week #32 Assessment

Circle the best answer.

1. What does manufacture mean?

   A. to write a letter

   B. to play a computer game

   C. to make something in a factory

2. What two things might you need to manufacture a desk?

   A. soil and grass

   B. wood and screws

   C. glass and string

3. Draw something that is manufactured.

4. Toys and games are manufactured. Explain how to play your favorite toy or game.

   ____

   ____

   ____

   ____

 1.W.2, 1.L.1, 1.L.6, 1.OA.D.8

Name____________________

Week #33

Write the number that is 10 more than each number shown.

1. 74 ______ 2. 68 ______

Day 1

Emma woke up. She was still tired. She had not slept very well. She got out of bed and put on her slippers. She walked to the bathroom. She got her toothbrush and put toothpaste on it. She began to brush her teeth. She looked in the mirror. She was surprised!

1. How did Emma feel when she woke up? ____________________
2. What did she do first when she got out of bed? ____________________
3. What did she do in the bathroom? ____________________
4. Why do you think Emma was surprised? ____________________

Day 2

Circle **true** or **false** for each sentence.

1. Water shapes the land. true false
2. Household products are sometimes made from rocks and minerals. true false
3. There is only one kind of soil. true false

Day 3

A flag can be a symbol for a country. Look at the American flag.

1. How many dark stripes do you count? __________
2. How many white stripes do you count? __________
3. Name one place you have seen the American flag. ____________________

Day 4

Name_______________________________________

1. Write the number that is 10 more than the number shown.

   62 _________ 58 _________

2. Fill in the chart. Below each number, write the number that is 10 more.

12	23	37	65

3. Xander played 8 computer games this week. He played 7 computer games last week. How many computer games did Xander play altogether?

   ____

4. Tell about a computer game you like to play. Explain why you like it.

   ____

   ____

   ____

   ____

   ____

Name________________________________

Week #34

Day 1

1. 13 + 3 = ____

2. 69 + 4 = ____

Day 2

1. Sight words are words you see often. Write the sight words in ABC order.

ask	have	just	give	after

__________ __________ __________ __________ __________

The letter **c** has two sounds. There is a soft **c** (**/s/**) as in **ice** and a hard **c** (**/k/**) as in **case**.
Read each word. Write **soft** or **hard** for the **c** you hear.

2. cent ______________ 3. coat ______________

Day 3

Circle the correct word to complete each sentence.

1. Earth's surface is mostly made up of ____________(land, water).
2. Most of Earth's water is ______________(salty, freshwater).
3. Some of Earth's water cannot be used because it is ______________(frozen, fresh).
4. Water found beneath Earth's surface is called ______________(groundwater, tap water).

Day 4

A **pledge** is a serious promise. An **allegiance** is a feeling of loyalty. The Pledge of Allegiance is a pledge that is said to the American flag.

1. What does **pledge** mean? ______________________
2. What does **allegiance** mean? ______________________
3. What is one thing you could make a serious promise to?

____

Name____

1. Place the sight words in ABC order on each train.

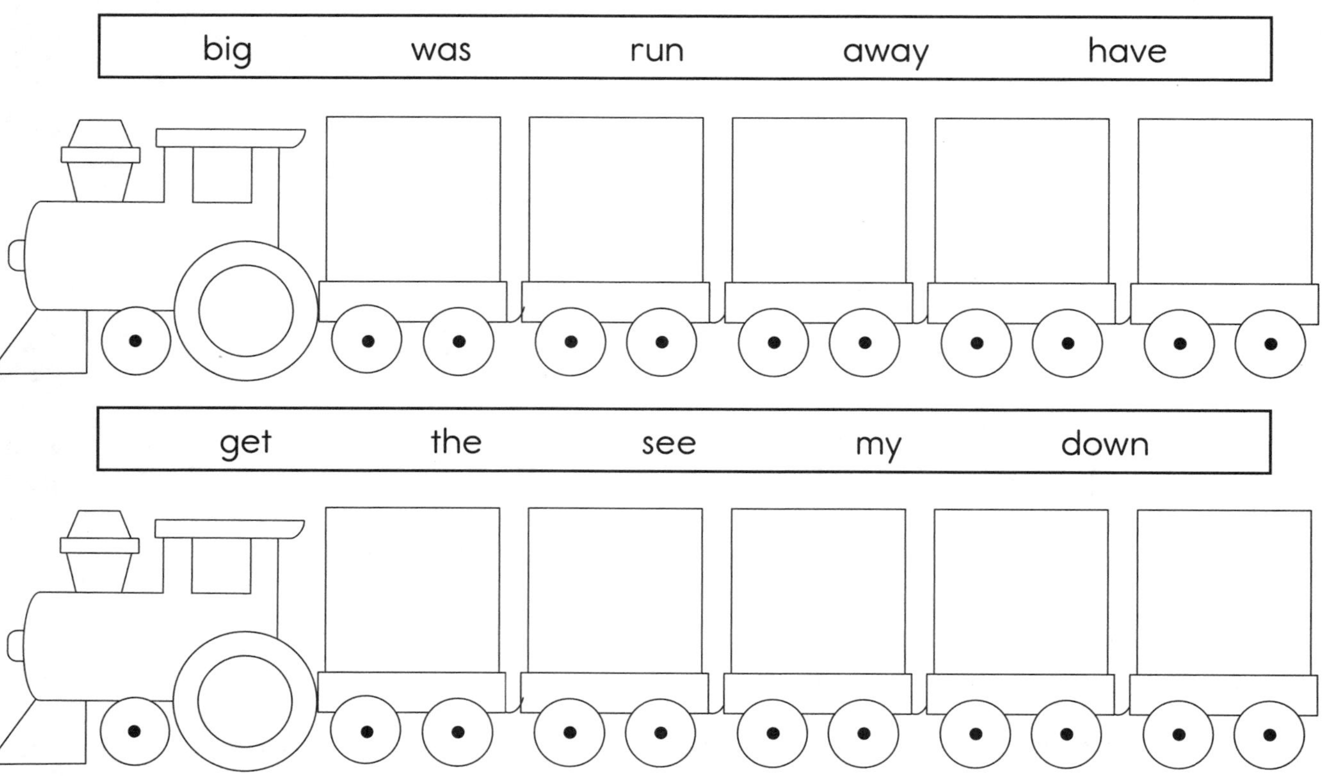

2. Think about the sound a train makes as it chugs along the tracks. If a train could talk, what do you think it would say? After you have written your sentences, type them on a computer. Share your story with a friend.

____

____

____

____

____

____

____

____

____

Name____

Week #35

Day 1

1. Molly ate 4 cherries, 8 grapes, and 1 orange for breakfast. How many pieces of fruit did Molly eat in all?

   _____ + _____ + _____ = _____

   Molly ate _______ pieces of fruit in all.

Day 2

It is important to be safe when a tornado is near. The best place to be is in a basement. If no basement is available, it is best to go to the middle of a house or a building and to stay away from windows. If you are outside, it is best to go to a ditch or lie low on the ground.

1. Where is the best place to be? ____________________
2. Where should you go if no basement is available? ____________________
3. What should you stay away from? ____________________
4. Where should you go if you are outside? ____________________

Day 3

1. How can a computer be used as a science tool? Share your answer with a friend.

   ____

   ____

   ____

   ____

Day 4

The Statue of Liberty is a symbol of freedom. It is in New York Harbor. It shows friendship to all people who come to America. It was a gift from France.

1. Where is the Statue of Liberty? ____________________

   ____

2. What does it show? ____________________

3. Who gave the Statue of Liberty to America? ____________________

Name____

1. Write the letter to match the definition to the name of the computer part.

______ moved with your hand to control what is on the computer screen	A. keyboard
______ the screen of the computer	B. headphones
______ used to type words or numbers	C. monitor
______ worn over your ears to hear sounds on the computer	D. mouse

2. Which do you think is better?

   A. writing something by hand   B. writing something on the computer

3. What are two rules to follow when using a computer?

   ____

   ____

   ____

   ____

   ____

Name________________________________

1. 80 – 70 = ________

2. 60 – 30 = ________

Add the suffix **-er** or **-ful** to the end of each word.

1. thank__________
2. dream__________
3. harm__________
4. peace__________
5. call__________
6. truth__________
7. farm__________
8. sing__________

1. Pick a household object that could be improved. Draw and write about how you could make it better.

____

____

____

____

The White House is in Washington, DC. It is where the president and his family lives. It has 132 rooms. The White House has a bowling alley, a movie theater, and a tennis court.

1. Where is the White House? ________________________________
2. How many rooms does it have? ________________________________
3. Name three things the White House has.

____

Name____

1. Draw a picture of what you think the inside of the White House looks like. Include the movie theater and bowling alley in your drawing.

2. Would you like to live in the White House? Write two sentences that tell why or why not.

____

____

____

____

Name________________________________

Write the number that is 10 less than each number shown.

1. 88 _______
2. 76 _______

Day 1

Jose volunteers at an animal shelter. The shelter is full of dogs and cats. They are waiting to find loving homes. Jose takes care of the cats and the dogs. He feeds them. He gives them baths.

Retell the story in your own words. Write two or more sentences.

____

____

____

Day 2

1. Use the words from the word bank to complete the sentences.

bathing	brush	floss	throw away	wash

There are many ways to be healthy. For healthy gums and teeth, it is important to ________________and ________________your teeth every day. ________________your hands with soap and warm water to stay healthy. ________________ used tissues right away. ________________helps to keep your body clean.

Day 3

An **election** is the event where people vote to choose a leader. People **vote** with a special piece of paper. This paper is called a **ballot**. Draw a line to match each word to its meaning.

1. vote
2. ballot
3. election

A. a special piece of paper
B. the event where people vote
C. to choose a leader

Day 4

Name____________________________________

1. Write the number that is 10 less than the number shown.

   62 __________ 36 __________

2. Fill in the chart. Below each number, write the number that is 10 less.

15	28	42	59

3. At the pet store, 6 hamsters, 7 fish, and 2 lizards are for sale. How many pets are for sale at the pet store?

   At the pet store, _________ pets are for sale.

4. Do you have a pet? Tell about your pet or a pet you have known. Read your story to your classmates and answer their questions.

   ____

   ____

   ____

   ____

   ____

Name______________________________

Day 1

1. Look at the tally chart. How many more children like pepperoni pizza than mushroom pizza?

Favorite Pizza		
Pepperoni	Mushroom	Cheese
||||	||	|||

Pepperoni is liked by______ more children.

Day 2

A **digraph** is two letters that make a new sound. **Ch-** is a digraph. Add **ch-** to complete each word. Write the word.

1. _____ ip ______________________
2. _____ op ______________________
3. _____ in ______________________

Synonyms are words that have the same meaning. Match the synonyms.

4. paste   hope
5. wish   glue
6. like   enjoy

Day 3

1. Draw a circle around each item that comes mainly from plants.
2. Draw a triangle around each item that comes mainly from animals.

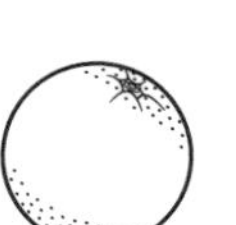

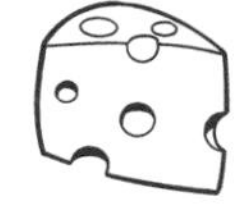

Day 4

A **constitution** is a list of rules. The Constitution of the United States was written to tell US citizens what the laws in America are.

1. Write a constitution, or a list of rules, for your classroom.

____

____

____

____

Name________________________________

Week #38 Assessment

1. Write the missing digraph to complete each word.

ch	sh	th	wh

Kelly brought a cat home from the pet _____op.

Jordan made a sandwich with meat and _____eese.

Tell me _____ere you found it.

Remember to say _____ank you.

2. Draw a line to match each adjective to the stronger adjective.

sad	nice
high	unhappy
kind	tall

3. Think about a time when a friend, a teacher, or someone in your family was kind to you. Tell what that person did and how it made you feel. Give your story a title.

____

____

____

____

____

____

____

Name________________________________

Week #40

Day 1

1. How many nails long is the hammer?

The hammer is ______ nails long.

Day 2

When you edit a sentence, you correct it.
Rewrite each sentence. Correct three mistakes in each one.

1. mariah wants two get a new pet

____

2. her Aunt lisa does not want a cat or a dog

____

3. maybe they con get a fish

____

4. fish are easy to take cure of

____

Day 3

1. Give an example of something you can recycle.

____

2. Give an example of something you cannot recycle.

____

Day 4

Inventions are new ideas to solve problems. The first erasers were made of bread. Today, they are made of rubber. The first toothbrushes were made of twigs. They looked like stiff paintbrushes. Today, they are made of nylon.

1. What are **inventions**? ______________________

2. What were the first erasers made of? ______________________

3. What were the first toothbrushes made of? ______________________

Name____

1. Think of a problem you have. Then, draw an invention to solve your problem.

2. Write instructions explaining how to use your invention.

____

____

____

____

____

____

Answer Key

Page 9
Day 1: 1. 25; **Day 2:** 1. Ms. Wolf; 2. read, write, do math; 3. be kind and listen;
4. when the class is too noisy; **Day 3:** 1. D;
2. C; 3. B; 4. A; **Day 4:** 1. Drawings will vary.
2. Answers will vary.

Page 10
1. 17; 2. 23; 3. Answers will vary. 4. Answers will vary but should include a logical reason and sequence of events.

Page 11
Day 1: 1. 9; 2. 8; **Day 2:** 1. My; 2. (circled) cat picture; 3. Check students' period placement. 4. cat, bath; **Day 3:** 1. Can Fly; 2. Cannot Fly; **Day 4:** 1. Drawings and answers will vary.

Page 12
1. She, Peter; 2. Check students' period placement. 3. nap, leg; 4. Answers will vary.
5. Answers will vary.

Page 13
Day 1: 1. 6; **Day 2:** 1. play; 2. make shapes on a wall; 3. Answers will vary.
Day 3: 1. Answers will vary but may include a ruler, yardstick, meterstick, or tape measure. B. balance scale; C. thermometer; D. clock, stopwatch, or timer;
Day 4: 1. past, present; 2. Answers will vary but may include clothes and writing tools.

Page 14
1. Answers will vary but may include a ruler, yardstick, meterstick, or tape measure.
2. Answers will vary but may include a ruler, yardstick, meterstick, or tape measure.
3. Answers will vary. 4. Answers and drawings will vary.

Page 15
Day 1: 1. 20; **Day 2:** 1. Nouns will vary.
2. animals, bears, boys, girls; **Day 3:** 1. Does salt water or freshwater freeze faster?
2. a container of saltwater, a container of freshwater, a freezer, and a timer;
3. Answers will vary. **Day 4:** 1. Drawings will vary. 2. Answers will vary.

Page 16
1. A community is a place where people work and play. 2. Answers will vary.
3. Drawings will vary. 4. Answers will vary.

Page 17
Day 1: 1. 18; 2. 16; **Day 2:** 1. many people in the world; 2. in ponds; 3. rain; 4. Answers will vary. **Day 3:** 1. B; 2. C; 3. A; 4. D;
Day 4: 1. circled: police officer and firefighter; triangle: nurse and doctor

Page 18
1. 9, 18, 5; 2. 11, 13; 3. 14; 4. Answers will vary.

Page 19
Day 1: 1. true; **Day 2:** 1. Pascal, Virginia, Walsh, Utah; 2. ripe, pine, dime, bite;
Day 3: 1. smell; 2. see; 3. hear; 4. taste;
5. touch; **Day 4:** 1. Check students' drawings.

Page 20
1. Kit, Kit, Fluffy, Fluffy, Kit, Fluffy, Kit;
2. Kit, Fluffy; 3. Because they are the names of a particular person and a particular cat. 4. Answers will vary. Provide research assistance for students who do not know the meaning of their names.

Answer Key

Page 21
Day 1: 1. 8:30; **Day 2:** 1. in the ocean; 2. for thousands of years; 3. more than 350 kinds; 4. big or small; **Day 3:** 1. telescope, pencil, camera, notebook; **Day 4:** 1. no check; 2. check; 3. check; 4. no check

Page 22
1. C; 2. Answers will vary but should be a complete and relevant question. 3. Answers will vary.

Page 23
Day 1: 1. twenty-eight, 28; fourteen, 14; five, 5; **Day 2:** 1. rides; 2. smells; 3. holds; 4. sees; 5–8. bl; **Day 3:** 1. O; 2. F; 3. F; 4. O; **Day 4:** 1. Right: play, read; Responsibility: follow rules, learn

Page 24
1. right; 2. responsibility; 3. right; 4. responsibility; 5. Drawings will vary. 6. Answers will vary.

Page 25
Day 1: 1. 3; **Day 2:** 1. ride a horse; 2. horse books; 3. in art class; 4. Answers will vary. **Day 3:** 1. Answers will vary. **Day 4:** 1. Drawings will vary. 2. Answers will vary.

Page 26
1. 5; 2. 7; 3. Answers will vary but should relate to the story and show a logical connection between the first and last part of the sentence.

Page 27
Day 1: 1. 7; 2. 6; **Day 2:** 1. fire; 2. Answers will vary but may include round or bouncy. 3. Answers will vary but may include *play, pay, May, say, lay way stayay, Fay, ray*, or *bay*. Check students' circling. **Day 3:** 1. C; 2. N—does not have four legs, fur, or whiskers; 3. N—does not have fur or whiskers; **Day 4:** 1. January; 2. Friday; 3. December; 4. Saturday

Page 28
1. tall, tree; cold, snowman; slow, turtle; fast, rabbit; 2. Check students' circling. 3. Answers will vary but should include an adjective.

Page 29
Day 1: 1. 7; 2. 10; **Day 2:** 1. a large bird; 2. up to nine feet; 3. a man; 4. It is too big. **Day 3:** 1. All images should be circled. **Day 4:** 1. Drawings will vary. 2. Answers will vary.

Page 30
1. B, C, A, D; 2. Answers will vary. 3. Answers will vary. 4. Answers will vary but should describe various similar properties of matter.

Page 31
Day 1: 1. 8; 2. 9; **Day 2:** 1. o; 2. don't; 3. Answers will vary but may include *pow, vow, bow, how, sow, cow*, and *wow*. 4. circle pictures: owl, cow; **Day 3:** 1. liquid; 2. solid; 3. gas; **Day 4:** 1. sickness, crowded, bad storms; 2. two months

Answer Key

Page 32
1. *Mayflower*; 2. months; 3. food; 4. sick; 5. Drawings will vary. 6. Answers will vary.

Page 33
Day 1: 1. 14; 2. 11; **Day 2:** 1. if she could have a teacher; 2. how to act and have fun onstage; 3. called an acting teacher; 4. Ming was happy!; **Day 3:** 1. A; 2. C; 3. B; **Day 4:** 1. Drawings will vary. 2. Drawings will vary.

Page 34
1. 15; 2. 8; 3. 14; 4. Answers will vary.

Page 35
Day 1: 1. 18; 2. 11; **Day 2:** 1. Answers will vary but may include tiny or miniature.
2. phone or bell sound; **Day 3:** 1. i, t (Light); 2. t (Heat); 3. o, u (Sound); **Day 4:** 1. Drawings will vary. 2. Answers will vary.

Page 36
1. soft, fluffy; hot, burning; tall, giant; pretty, beautiful; 2. A. to shut; B. to make a boat move in water; C. a place with grass and trees to play or hike; 3. Answers will vary but should include at least three adjectives.

Page 37
Day 1: 1. 7; **Day 2:** 1. holes in the trees; 2. hang buckets on the trees; 3. metal; 4. at the end of the day; **Day 3:** 1. cheetah; 2. sphere; 3. empty wagon; **Day 4:** 1. Check students' matching.

Page 38
1. Drawings will vary but should show an *F* or an *S* at the appropriate spots.
2. Answers will vary. 3. Answers will vary.

Page 39
Day 1: 1. Answers will vary but may include . **Day 2:** 1. Answers will vary. 2. kick, will kick; 3. bake, will bake; **Day 3:** 1. A. pull; B. push; C. pull; D. push; **Day 4:** 1. kind words; 2. together fairly

Page 40
1. nice, gentle, fair, caring; 2. Answers will vary but may include that everyone gets the same amount of something. 3. Drawings will vary. 4. Answers will vary.

Page 41
Day 1: 1. 8; **Day 2:** 1. Japan; 2. 17; 3. three; **Day 3:** 1. Gravity, Earth; 2. down; 3. moon; **Day 4:** 1. globe; 2. map; 3. Answers will vary but may include countries, continents, or the world.

Page 42
1. 8 + 2 = 10, 9 + 6 = 15, 2 + 2 = 4; 1 + 2 = 3, 6 + 7 = 13, 5 + 6 = 11; 2. Answers will vary. 3. Answers will vary. If possible, make a computer available. If not, help students to copy and share their work.

Page 43
Day 1: 1. 1, 2, 3; **Day 2:** 1–3. An exclamation point should be added to the end of each sentence. 4. backpack; 5. sunshine; **Day 3:** 1. Answers will vary. 2. They are made of metal. **Day 4:** 1. map; 2. a town; 3. two; 4. yes

Answer Key

Page 44
1. An exclamation point should be placed at the end of each sentence. 2. cannot; skateboard; afternoon; forget; 3. Answers will vary but one sentence should describe a feeling and end with an exclamation point.

Page 45
Day 1: 1. 11; 2. 9; **Day 2:** 1. She needed help. 2. It helps her walk. 3. They help her see. 4. It helps her hear. **Day 3:** 1. N; 2. L; 3. L; 4. L; 5. N; 6. N; **Day 4:** 1. map; 2. globe; 3. map; 4. globe; 5. map

Page 46
1. circled: child, fish, seal, tree, crab;
2. Answers will vary but should include a characteristic of a living thing. 3. Answers will vary but should include a characteristic of a nonliving thing.

Page 47
Day 1: 1. Answers will vary but may include [Happy Birthday]. **Day 2:** 1. mp; Answers will vary but may include *lump* or *jump*. 2. mp; Answers will vary but may include *damp*, *lamp*, or *ramp*. Check students' circling.
Day 3: 1. apple tree, grass, sunflower, lettuce; 2. Answers will vary.
Day 4: 1–4. Answers will vary.

Page 48
1. N W E S; 2. B; 3. A; 4. Answers will vary.

Page 49
Day 1: 1. 12; **Day 2:** 1. Europe; 2. more than 100 years ago; 3. forests; 4. hide in warm places, rest under rocks and logs;
Day 3: 1. birds, turtles; 2. bats, birds;
Day 4: 1. urban; 2. rural; 3. urban; 4. rural; 5. Answers will vary.

Page 50
1. 13; 2. 11; 3. Answers will vary. 4. Answers will vary.

Page 51
Day 1: 1. 2 tens, 1 one; **Day 2:** 1–2. Answers will vary. 3. Check students' circling. **Day 3:** 1. true; 2. true; 3. true; **Day 4:** 1–3. Check students' coloring.

Page 52
1. ant, aunt; wrap, rap; hi, high; buy, by; 2-4. Check students' circling. 5. Answers will vary but the second sentence should include a pair of homophones and be written with peer support.

Page 53
Day 1: 1. 29; 2. 36; **Day 2:** 1. in a big room, his attic; 2. dark and dusty; 3. webs; 4. a light;
Day 3: 1. bee; 2. Flowers; 3. birds; 4. Skunks;
Day 4: 1. cactus, spiders, snakes; 2. trees, snow, bears, skiers; 3. green plants, frogs, monkeys

Answer Key

Page 54
1. B, D, A, C; 2. Drawings will vary but should show something green where an insect could hide. 3. Answers will vary but the writing should show an understanding of camouflage.

Page 55
Day 1: 1. >; 2. =; **Day 2:** 1. Answers will vary. **Day 3:** 1. A. 2. C; 3. B; **Day 4:** 1. pencil, park bench, paper; 2. Answers will vary but may include a house.

Page 56
1. B; 2. C; 3. Drawings will vary. 4. Answers will vary. Monitor students' responses.

Page 57
Day 1: 1. 6; **Day 2:** 1. a big pile of waste; 2. trash, paper, plastic; 3. gas; 4. The waste is used again. **Day 3:** 1. tundra; 2. desert; 3. rain forest; **Day 4:** 1. Drawings will vary but should include recyclable items such as paper, glass, and cans. 2. Answers will vary.

Page 58
1. 11; 2. 69, 57; 3. B; 4. Answers will vary but should relate to the question and show a logical connection between the first and last part of the sentence.

Page 59
Day 1: 1. 29; 2. 36; **Day 2:** 1. dis-, not; un-, not; re-, again; pre-, before; **Day 3:** 1. 2, 1, 5, 3, 4; **Day 4:** 1. Drawings will vary. 2. Answers will vary.

Page 60
1. to heat before; 2. to not like something; 3. to play again; 4. not happy; 5. Answers will vary. Monitor students' responses. Encourage revision if needed.

Page 61
Day 1: 1. 6; **Day 2:** 1. a cat. 2. tosses it up; 3. when Josie brushes his fur; **Day 3:** 1. bones; 2. muscles; 3. lungs; 4. heart; **Day 4:** 1. Both: fair, peaceful; Abraham Lincoln: president; Martin Luther King Jr.: preacher

Page 62
1. A. nose; B. eye; C. elbow; D. hand; E. knee; F. foot; 2. Answers will vary but may include height, hair, feet, or fingernails.

Page 63
Day 1: 1. 6:30; **Day 2:** 1. March; 2. February; 3. Thursday; 4. Saturday; 5–6. Students should add a question mark at the end of each sentence. **Day 3:** 1. F; 2. F; 3. T; 4. T; **Day 4:** 1. W; 2. N; 3. W; 4. N; 5. N; 6. W; 7. N; 8. W

Page 64
1. C; 2. A; 3. Drawings will vary. 4. Drawings will vary. 5. Answers will vary but may include water, flashlight, a tent, and food.

Page 65
Day 1: 1. 4; **Day 2:** 1. England; 2. to be brushed often; 3. to work; 4. to play and run outside; **Day 3:** 1. winter; 2. summer; 3. autumn; 4. spring; **Day 4:** 1. good; 2. service; 3. service; 4. good

Answer Key

Page 66
1. brown; 2. Sam; 3. 19; 4. Answers will vary.

Page 67
Day 1: 1. 1 ten, 5 ones; 2. 2 tens, 3 ones; **Day 2:** 1. flew; 2. stew; 3. grew; 4. Stan's; 5. dad's; 6. Mom's; **Day 3:** 1. i (light); 2. e, a (heat); 3. o, o (food); 4. o, e (computers); **Day 4:** 1. Drawings will vary. 2. Drawings will vary.

Page 68
1. dew, flew; 2. blue, glue; 3. mood, tool; 4. look, took; 5. Colby's, Arifa's, Lola's; 6. Stories will vary but should include information gathered from a friend.

Page 69
Day 1: 1. 6 + 6 + 4 = 16, 16; **Day 2:** 1. It flew into a tree. 2. helped Bridget; 3. tug at the string; 4. windy; **Day 3:** 1. one; 2. Answers will vary but may include round, white, and bright. **Day 4:** 1. 3, 1, 2

Page 70
1. C; 2. D; 3. Answers will vary but should include an opinion and reason(s).

Page 71
Day 1: 1. 16; 2. 6; **Day 2:** 1. to; 2. two; 3. too; 4. It; 5. He; **Day 3:** 1. Answers will vary. **Day 4:** 1. desk, dice, diving board, doughnuts; 2. Answers will vary but may include paper or pencils.

Page 72
1. C; 2. B; 3. Drawings will vary.
4. Explanations will vary.

Page 73
Day 1: 1. 84; 2. 78; **Day 2:** 1. tired; 2. put on her slippers; 3. got her toothbrush and put toothpaste on it; 4. Answers will vary.
Day 3: 1. true; 2. true; 3. false; **Day 4:** 1. 7; 2. 6; 3. Answers will vary but may include school or sporting events.

Page 74
1. 72, 68; 2. 22, 33, 47, 75; 3. 15 games; 4. Answers will vary but should include an opinion and reason(s).

Page 75
Day 1: 1. 16; 2. 73; **Day 2:** 1. after, ask, give, have, just; 2. soft *c*; 3. hard *c*;
Day 3: 1. water; 2. salty; 3. frozen; 4. groundwater; **Day 4:** 1. a serious promise; 2. a feeling of loyalty; 3. Answers will vary but may include school or family.

Page 76
1. away, big, have, run, was; 2. down, get, my, see, the; 3. Answers will vary. If possible, make a computer available. If not, help students to copy and share their work.

Page 77
Day 1: 1. 4 + 8 + 1 = 13, 13;
Day 2: 1. a basement; 2. middle of a house or a building; 3. windows; 4. a ditch or lie low on ground; **Day 3:** Answers will vary but may include to store data, create graphs, and do research. **Day 4:** 1. New York Harbor; 2. freedom or friendship; 3. France

Page 78
1. D, C, A, B; 2. Answers will vary. 3. Answers will vary but may include not having food or drink near a computer.

Page 79
Day 1: 1. 10; 2. 30; **Day 2:** 1. ful; 2. er; 3. ful; 4. ful; 5. er; 6. ful; 7. er; 8. er;
Day 3: 1. Answers and drawings will vary.
Day 4: 1. Washington, DC; 2. 132 rooms; 3. movie theater, bowling alley, tennis court

Page 80
1. Drawings will vary. 2. Answers will vary.

Page 81
Day 1: 1. 78; 2. 66; **Day 2:** 1. Answers will vary. **Day 3:** 1. brush, floss, Wash, Throw away, Bathing; **Day 4:** 1. C; 2. A; 3. B

Page 82
1. 52, 26; 2. 5, 18, 32, 49; 3. 15; 4. Answers will vary. Monitor students' responses.

Page 83
Day 1: 1. 2; **Day 2:** 1. chip; 2. chop; 3. chin; 4. glue; 5. hope; 6. enjoy;
Day 3: 1. circled: books, orange, tea; 2. triangle: butter, cheese, can of tuna;
Day 4: 1. Answers will vary.

Page 84
1. shop, cheese, where, thank; 2. sad, unhappy; high, tall; kind, nice; 3. Stories will vary but should tell about an event of kindness and have an appropriate title.

Page 85
Day 1: 1. 10; 2. 7; **Day 2:** 1. He didn't want to do chores. 2. He thought they were not fun. 3. play outside; 4. his friends; **Day 3:** 1. air; 2. water; 3. land; **Day 4:** 1. Time lines will vary.

Page 86
1. A, B, C, D; 4; 2. Drawings will vary but should convey an environmental message. 3. Answers will vary but should focus on one of the items in the picture.

Page 87
Day 1: 1. 8; **Day 2:** 1. Mariah wants to get a new pet. 2. Her Aunt Lisa does not want a cat or a dog. 3. Maybe they can get a fish. 4. Fish are easy to take care of.
Day 3: 1. Answers will vary but may include paper, plastic, glass, and metal. 2. Answers will vary but may include food scraps, certain plastics, and foam takeout boxes.
Day 4: 1. Inventions are new ideas to solve problems. 2. bread; 3. twigs

Page 88
1. Drawings will vary. 2. Answers will vary.

Notes